Rebuilding Your Life

After Grief and Loss

Bruce Goettsche

Rebuilding Your Life After Grief and Loss

Scripture quotations are taken from the Holy Bible, New Living Translation, copyright ©1996, 2004, 2007, 2013 by Tyndale House Foundation. Used by permission of Tyndale House Publishers, Inc., Carol Stream, Illinois 60188. All rights reserved.

Cover Picture: With thanks to the team from One Family, One Purpose for allowing me to use this photo. Check them out at http://www.onefamilyonepurpose.org/

©2016 by Bruce Goettsche
Rebuilding Your Life After Grief and Loss
All rights reserved.

ISBN: 9781533003539
ISBN 153300353X

Rebuilding Your Life After Grief and Loss

Dedicated to Mom and Dad

and the many others

I look forward to greeting at the

Great Reunion with the Lord

Rebuilding Your Life After Grief and Loss

Rebuilding Your Life After Grief and Loss

Table of Contents

Introduction   1

1- Why Can't I Get Through This?   5

2- The Cycle of Grief   17

3- Special Circumstances   33

4- Getting Help   47

5- Re-Purpose Difficult Days   55

6- Build on What You Are Learning   63

7- Building Memories While You Can   69

8- Pay a Dividend   77

9- Nagging Questions   81

10- Concluding Thoughts   97

11- To the Reader   101

Introduction

If you dare to love, you will inevitably experience the pain of grief and loss. People die. Relationships end. Jobs are terminated, and retirement ages are enforced. Tragedies take place. Relocation forces us to leave familiar places and friends. And when any of these things happen, the person who dares to love feels the loss intensely. We call this grief.

I have known loss. My father died by inches because of Alzheimer's disease. We grieved for him for years as we watched him slowly lose become merely a shell of the man he was. My mother died suddenly and the grief from her death was painful in a very different way. I have also experienced the still different grief and sense of rejection and failure that comes with divorce.

Pastors grieve when they must leave the church they have been serving. People grieve when a job they loved is lost to downsizing. We grieve when a favorite landmark or restaurant is torn down. We grieve when we lose our home to tragedy or out of financial necessity. We grieve when something happens that changes everything in one quick moment. Grief is all around us.

The principles you will find in this book can all be applied to all kinds of grief. My primary focus will be the grief that comes with the death of a loved one.

Each year for the last decade I have spoken at a Hospice Survivors Service of Remembrance. I have listened to the grief-filled stories of people that attend these meetings. As a Pastor, I've sat with hundreds of family members who are grieving. As we sit and visit in preparation for a funeral I have listened not only with my ears but also my heart and I have witnessed emotions that cover the spectrum. I don't write as a theoretician, I write, I hope, as a friend who has traveled a similar road to you.

Loss can debilitate. Some people are paralyzed because of loss. This is especially true when the loss is tragic. They seem to get "stuck." They just can't seem to move on after the loss. I've seen other people who seemed to get over the loss almost too quickly. Grief is strange, and it affects different people in different ways.

Rebuilding Your Life After Grief and Loss

There are lots of good books on grief. I hope this will be one of them. I have longed for a resource to give people that speaks practically, giving concrete and practical strategies to help people navigate this rough and winding road called grief so they can return to living the life yet before them.

My primary goal is to help you to understand, embrace, and cope with loss. Loss leaves us wondering, "What can I do?" We feel helpless, empty, numb. We desperately want help, but we feel those around us stop caring before we have healed. (I will point out that this is how you feel . . . it isn't always the truth.")

I also want to take this one step further. I want to suggest ways to learn from this time of loss and use it to strengthen and enrich the remainder of your life. Loss leaves a hole in our soul. At the same time loss is one of the best instructors for learning what is truly important in life. I hope to help you take steps to rebuild and allow the loss of the person you loved to pay rich dividends in your future.

You will read the stories of many different people in this book. I am indebted to the many families who have allowed me to share in their time of loss. I always learn something from every family I visit. Some of what I have gained has changed my life. I share these lessons with profound gratitude.

My prayer is that you will find comfort and hope in these words. I know that I do not understand your unique situation. However, I hope there will be something here that will bring you comfort and understanding. I pray these words will help you to develop a new compassion for and understanding of others who are grieving. And, by God's grace, I hope you find the help you need to continue to live while you are alive. Even with a broken heart.

1
Why Can't I Get Through This?

After any kind of loss there will be pain. After a few weeks of battling the numbness and grief you may begin to wonder why you can't move on with your life. Why does it feel so wrong that the rest of the world is moving on while your world seems to have stopped? Then, when you feel you have started to move on, grief sneaks up on you and ambushes you. Sometimes you feel like you are a terrible person because you are moving on with life. You may even feel guilty if you laugh.

Sometimes even our faith complicates things. We believe (we hope) that the person we loved "lives even though they die" (see John 11 in the Bible). We know we should be happy for the person who has been delivered from the broken shell of their body. There is a sense in which we feel the person of faith "should be over the grief by now." So, we say faithful things ("I know they are in a better place" and "I know someday we will see each other again." Or "I bet there is a great reunion taking place in Heaven.") We feel we have to hide the devastating sense of loss that resides within us. In addition to the pain of loss we also feel guilty for our seeming lack of faith.

The notion that God wants us to act like death is "no big deal" is wrong. Death was never part of God's plan. Death entered the world as a consequence of sin. When we grieve the loss of someone we should also be grieving the corruption of this world which brings about death.

Grief is complex. When someone dies there are many companion losses.

Let me give you some examples. If you lost a parent you also lost a counselor, a mentor, the leader of the family. No more phone calls. Family dinners will never be the same. You may have lost your parent as a babysitter. You may have lost the person you dreamt would walk you down the aisle, help you plan your wedding, or teach you how to care for your sick baby. You have lost that special person who was your rock when life was difficult. You may even find that you miss the wild idiosyncrasies that made your parent a unique individual. Your dynamics with your siblings may change (especially if there is an estate that is contested).

If you lose a sibling, you experience a fracture in the family that will never be able to heal. You have lost a treasured companion who understood you as no one else could. You lost some of those memories that only the two of you shared. You lost that aunt or uncle that would bless your children. You lost someone you could always count on.

If you lose a spouse, you also lose your roommate, your lover, and your traveling companion. You may have lost the person who paid the bills, washed the clothes, cooked the meals, took care of repairs, cared for the children. You may have lost a significant part of your income. You lost the one person who made you feel more alive than anyone else. You lost what is likely your best friend in the world. You lost your dreams of your future together. You lost your partner who you hoped would walk with you as you grew older.

If you lose a child, the loss is almost too much to bear. Not only do you miss the hugs and the joy of watching your child, you also lose all the things you dreamt of enjoying. You may have lost those precious moments when you lay with your child in your arms and feel that sense that "all is right with the world." You lost your dreams of seeing that child walk, go to school, graduate, get married, and become a parent. You have lost the enjoyment of the sporting events or extracurricular activities in which they would have participated. You have lost the treasure of seeing what they would become. You have lost the friendship with your child that comes when they reach a certain age. You have lost that one who would care for you when you are older. You have lost out on their friends (and their parents) that you would have known and the grand-kids you would have enjoyed.

In case of a stillborn birth or a miscarriage you lost the chance to even meet your child. Some may say something ridiculous like, "At least you didn't get to know them." But that is precisely the problem! You became invested in that child the moment you learned you were going to have a child. You lost the chance to express your love to them. You have been deprived an opportunity to see their personality. You have lost out on the joy that you thought being pregnant would bring. And in some cases. you also lose out on the sympathy that other loses bring because somehow your loss is diminished because your child was not born alive.

If you lose a friend, you may have lost a traveling companion. You lost those friendly or fun texts and phone calls. You lost a confidant. You lost a person who appreciated you in a way others do not. No more hanging out with each other, so some of your social life is lost. The gathering of friends will have changed forever. There is an empty place in your life you cannot fill.

―――

I hope you get the point. Grief is difficult because you are grieving many different things.

To make matters even more complicated the process is not the same for everyone. It differs depending on your personality, the nature of the loss, the closeness to the one who is gone, your own preparation for the loss and your level of faith (which I believe is exceedingly important).

If you had a strained relationship your loss will be different from one who had a close relationship with the one who died.

Grief is different depending on whether it is a sudden or slow death. People debate whether one kind of death is better than others. Neither is *better* than the other; it is just different.

When someone dies suddenly you reel from shock. You cry and weep. It seems so very unreal. There are things left unsaid and plans left unfulfilled. The last words will forever be etched in your heart. There are hundreds of questions you can't get answered. You start to call them on the phone or think about stopping to see them and you realize you cannot, because they are gone. The grief washes over you with new force every time the reality of loss comes back. It is very painful.

When someone dies of a long-term illness you may feel guilty that you feel a sense of relief that the suffering is over. Sometimes tears are hard to come by but that is only because you are pretty well cried out. You have been grieving for a long time. Sometimes you feel guilt at reaching the point where you can no longer care for the person you love at home.

The sad thing about a long-term illness is that the painful memories seem to devour the memories of healthy and vibrant times. In a sense you have lost your past. Financial resources are drained. The time of suffering is so seared into your brain that it seems like all you can remember. You welcome any positive memory.

My dad's Alzheimer's disease went on for ten years. It is many years later and I have a hard time remembering my dad healthy. The time of dad's demise was so intense that it overshadowed the good memories.

Sometimes people grieve over the loss of a pet or even the loss of their sports team more than they grieve for a person or family member. This is because the depth of grief varies depending on the emotional relationship you had with the one who died. Sometimes there is a deeper relationship with our pet (or team, or car) than with some people in our lives.

I loved my paternal Grandfather. He drove me to many of my early preaching locations. We shared some wonderful memories during those times. He died of lung cancer. It was not a pretty death.

One day many years later I was overwhelmed by the realization that I grieved the death of our family dog more intensely than I did my Grandfather. It seemed wrong. But it wasn't. The dog was attached to me. No matter what mood I was in my dog loved me. When I came home the dog greeted me with an enthusiasm that was unequaled. When I left home she always watched me, hopeful that I would take her along with me. It wasn't that I didn't love my Grandfather, I simply grieved differently because the loss of my dog was a greater personal loss. It is not right or wrong, it is just the way it is.

We make a serious mistake when we say to someone "I know how you feel." You have probably had people say this to you. Sometimes they tell you all about their personal loss. If they really knew how you felt they would know that you really don't want to hear about their losses. You are barely able to bear up under your own loss.

Though people may have similar experiences (losing a parent, a child, a friend) each relationship is different. We have greater empathy for people who have similar losses to us, but each loss is unique. We can learn from those who have had similar losses, but their understanding of our loss is limited.

It is important to keep the varieties of grief in mind even as you grieve in your family. It may seem as if someone in the family doesn't care because they are not grieving "as much" as someone else. You must remember that people grieve differently because of their: personality, their relationship with the person who died, the nature of the death was different. They may be in a different stage of grief than you are in.

When my father died my mother did not want to be there when he died. She didn't shed tears (in front of us) when he died. Some people said, "She is dealing with this so well." It would have been easy for my sisters and I to conclude that mom didn't love dad. How could mom not want to be with her husband? Why didn't she shed tears?

The thing is, my mom had been grieving for over ten years. She lost a little of dad every day. I cannot imagine how painful this was for her. She didn't cry because she didn't have any tears left. She couldn't be there when he died because she just could not bear that final "Good Bye." She seemed to be "doing well" because she was worn out. She was relieved that dad's suffering was finally over but that didn't mean she didn't miss her partner.

As the years went by it was obvious that mom was grieving. She frequently talked about how much she missed my dad. It seemed that the more time passed the more the grief surfaced. She shared many memories. As she remembered the good times it reminded her of what she had lost not only by dad's death, but also by his disease. She was alone, and it was painful. Part of her died with dad. It was important that people not draw the wrong conclusions from her immediate stoic appearance.

Don't assume that someone doesn't care because they grieve differently than you do. Each relationship is different. So is each person. Some grieve quietly. Some grieve with great expression. Some talk all the time about the person who died. Others seldom talk about their loss at all. Grief is like life. Different does not mean "better than" or "worse than" it just means different.

Billy Graham wrote a book titled *Nearing Home* and he talked about the pain of losing his wife Ruth.

He said he found himself grieving more as time went by. At first, he was grateful that she was no longer suffering. He rejoiced that she was with the Lord. However, as time passed he started to remember the things they did together. He started to forget the pain and started to miss the really good days they had together. This led to profound loneliness. He found himself missing his friend and companion. This is what we witnessed with my mom.

Grief will sneak up on you at odd times and in surprising places. It is impossible to put grief in a box and predict what it will do.

You don't have to apologize for your grief. It is better to own it. Embrace the fact that your grief shows that you had a significant relationship with someone. You hurt because you were blessed with a relationship that touched your heart.

Steps to Healing

It is important for you to stop and reflect on the depth of the loss you have experienced. Look at all the different losses that resulted from this one death. Make a list. Write down all the losses you can think of. Facing the real scope of the loss will help you. It will help you to understand why you feel such pain. It will help you to explain your pain to others and it will help you to give yourself the time you need to grieve.

It is going to take time to work through loss and rebuild your life. That is a natural and good thing. It is valuable to work at grief. Don't deny what is going on. Grief is necessary. Your grief is an indication that you loved.

When you find someone who will listen, talk about your pain. Work through this most difficult time with a friend or Pastor.

Pray. Ask God for His comfort and His strength. Read through the Psalms. Re-read 1 Corinthians 15. Seek His insight and His healing. He will be glad to give it.

Rebuilding Your Life After Grief and Loss

2
The Cycle of Grief

Elizabeth Kubler Ross is famous for having defined five stages of dying: Denial, Anger, Bargaining, Depression, and finally, Acceptance. She discovered that the same stages are found in grief. I find it best to think of the cycle this way: numbness, anger, depression, feeling lost, and then acceptance. This is important because if you understand the stages of grief it will help you navigate your way through the rough terrain of loss.

Numbness

When you first hear that someone has died or is dying often the first word you say is often, "No!" or "That can't be." Sometimes you simply stand speechless. At this time, you don't know what to say or how to feel. There is a part of you that feels this all must be a mistake. It is impossible to process the information. There is a paralyzing overload.

This is especially true in a tragic event. One-minute life is normal and good and suddenly *everything* has been turned upside down. It is impossible to comprehend what has just happened.

This was illustrated when as a country we watched with horror the terrorist attack on 9/11. We experienced a national time of denial. People stood in front of their televisions and were silent as the twin towers crumbled on live TV. The images were horrible but we could not pull ourselves away from the television as it was played over and over again. We struggled to find a way to comprehend such a horrible and senseless loss. When people were out and about everyone had a look of shock.

The same thing happens with our personal losses on a different scale. For a while (it could be weeks or longer) you will find yourself just "going through the motions." You don't seem to feel anything. You wonder how people can be so busy when your world seems to have stopped.

This numbness is actually a gift from God. It is God's way of helping you to cope with this rush of emotion. It is an emotional shock absorber.

It is quite common to feel numbness throughout the entire funeral process. People may misread this as indifference or that you are untouched by the loss. Some others may conclude you are "doing really well." The truth is that you have not even begun the grieving process yet. Your system is on overload and you are numb.

This numbness is what makes it possible for you to make decisions about burial, the funeral, and perhaps even a funeral meal. At the time of a death there are often lots of distractions. There is family, forgotten stories, visits from friends, and the preparation for the funeral itself. It is good to be numb . . . for a while. However, when the numbness passes you are often left with feelings of anger.

Anger

The anger you feel may be directed at many different things or people:
- You may find that you are angry at the person you blame for the death (as in a car accident or the person who committed the violent crime.) You may be angry at a manufacturer of a faulty product. In war, the President of the United States is often the focus of anger because of their position as Commander in Chief. Sometimes the focus of our anger has a face, sometimes it doesn't. Sometimes you may even be angry at

those who have come to help.

- You may be angry at the medical team because they didn't diagnose things earlier or didn't do enough or do it fast enough. You might even be angry at Doctors and the Nursing staff even for hurrying you through your "Good Byes." Your anger may express itself by a lawsuit designed to "punish" the person you deem responsible for the death.

- You may be angry at your family members who were not present or did not visit more often. You may be angry at family for decisions that were made that you feel hastened death. You may be angry at what someone in the family said, did, or didn't do or say.

- Your anger may be turned inward. You may be angry at yourself for not being more supportive, caring, or for not recognizing what you believe you should have seen. You may be angry at yourself because you think you should have been a better spouse, child, sibling, neighbor, friend or employee/employer. You may get angry with yourself for laughing or because for a few moments you seemed to forget the trauma of your loss. You may erroneously draw the conclusion that you are a horrible person to be so unaffected.

- You can even be angry at the person who died. You may be angry that they put off medical treatment or were too stubborn to go see the Doctor earlier. You may feel they did not fight hard enough. You may be angry because you feel they were reckless in their living which led to their death. You may even be angry that they died at an inopportune time (right before a wedding, graduation, birthday etc. "tarnishing the day").

- Often you are angry at circumstances. Why does one person walk away from a car accident while another person dies? Why do some babies die? Why did a gunman shoot someone you loved? It doesn't make any sense. You may be angry because, "it's not fair."

- It is common to be angry at God. You wonder why He "did this to you." Why would He take your loved one? Doesn't He know how much you needed them? It seems so unfair that others get to keep living their lives and your life seems to have stopped. Immediately after a loss we often ask ourselves "What did I do wrong that God is punishing me with such heartache?"

Please keep in mind is that this anger is normal. That does not excuse abusive words, or reckless actions; it simply explains the emotion you feel. We all want to make sense of loss somehow and one of the ways of doing this is to blame others.

It is important that we guard our tongue during this time. Sometimes words spoken will hurt long after the anger has subsided. Anger explains how you feel but it doesn't give you license to hurt others.

When you are angry at God you can be honest with Him. He is not put off by your questions or frustrations. Feel free to pour out your heart to Him. When you are ready and open to listen to Him you will find His comfort is great. He truly does understand your pain.

Depression

Once the anger starts to subside you may find you face a period of depression. Part of this depression is because the adrenalin that has been keeping you going, is now gone. As a result, you are tired and feel you don't have energy for anything. This is also the time when you often have to sort through belongings and deal with a host of legal matters. Sometimes there are expenses you don't know how to pay for. The loss takes on a new form in the way that it seems to simply suck the life right out of you. Each new task seems to bring more reasons for grief.

You may find yourself at times just sitting and staring. You may have the television on but you have no idea what you are watching. You may feel overwhelmed by everything that is going on around you. Tears (and sometimes sobbing) sneak up on you at odd moments. It is not uncommon to cry at a commercial or even at a song that plays on the radio.

It is sometimes hard to go back into the church after a death. Familiar songs bring tears. If the funeral was held in the church, you may find yourself reliving some of those events just by walking in the door.

You may need medical help and/or counseling. Your loss may be strangling you and you need help to function. Depression medicine does not have to be taken forever. Sometimes you can benefit from temporary assistance. Just as you might take an antibiotic for an infection, sometimes you may need help to battle emotional attacks as well.

Feeling Lost

After depression (and all these stages seem to be pretty fluid, you may move back and forth through these stages) there is often a period where you feel lost.

When my father died I could only describe the feeling as like a flag that had become partially detached from the pole and was flapping wildly in the wind. I felt lost. I was just flapping in the wind.

When my mother died it was like the flag was fully detached and blew away. One minute she was here the next minute she was not. I felt like an orphan; like I no longer belonged any place.

This sense of being lost comes because you are trying to process a new paradigm for your life. Everything has changed. You feel like you have lost your anchors and are adrift.

At this point you often realize that the reality of your own death has come much closer. As a result, some people act out by doing bizarre things (like they are trying to check items off of their bucket list), or they spend wild amounts of money. This is an attempt to find some feeling, some meaning, and some joy. There is a new fear that we will die before we feel we have lived.

During the time of being lost sometimes people

turn to the church while others drift away or turn to drugs or alcohol. Those who turn to the church realize that the question: "What happens after we die?" becomes intensely personal and relevant. If you don't already know the answer, you can look to the church to gain insight.

Though the church cannot answer the "Why?" questions, it can point you to a source of comfort and a group of people who will try to love you and help you through this time. If you hang in there you will eventually hear some of the eternal truth that will give you that anchor that you need.

Acceptance

Saying we get to a point of acceptance is somewhat of a misnomer. This doesn't mean that we are "fine." It only means that we recognize that our loved one is gone and is not coming back. We will not see them again until we (hopefully) are reunited in Heaven.

When you reach the point of acceptance life starts to look normal again. Normal is redefined. You must begin the process of living life without the person you loved. The grief will still come and go but when it comes you are better at coping with it. The periods of sadness are of shorter duration. You begin to live again. There is part of you that is missing but you know now that you are going to survive.

The grieving process is extensive. It takes time. Working through your grief is not something that will take only a few weeks.

> The reality is that you will grieve forever. You will not "get over" the loss of a loved one; you will learn to live with it. You will heal, and you will rebuild yourself around the loss you have suffered. You will be whole again, but you will never be the same. Nor should you be the same, nor would you want to.

> The time we take following a loss is important in grief and grieving as well as in healing. This gift of grief represents a completion of a connection we will never forget. A time of reflection, pain, despair, tragedy, hope, readjustment, re-involvement, and healing.[1]

I don't say this to discourage you. On the

---

[1] Elisabeth Kubler Ross and David Kessler, On Grief and Grieving: Finding the Meaning of Grief Through the Five Stages of Loss p. 230

contrary, you need to have realistic expectations and give yourself time to grieve.

Steps to Healing

What stage of grief do you feel you are in at present? It is helpful to remind yourself that these stages are all normal. By identifying where you are will help you to understand some of what is happening. You can share this with others, ("Right now I guess I am just in that sad and lonely stage").

I encourage you to gather with family and friends to talk about where each of you is in the process of grieving. If you are honest, others will tend to be honest. You won't all be in the same spot (this is so important to remember!) but you may be able to help each other work through these different phases of grief.

Your goal is to reach the point where you can move from mourning the death of your loved one and start celebrating their life. Grief is a process and it will take time. Often it takes a couple of years to grieve fully. That's something we must continue to stress to ourselves and to others.

The goal is to remember that the person who died also lived! Part of this process is the laughter that comes from recounting the great stories of a person's life. It is fun to do this in a group. One story tends to lead to another and then another. You may learn things you didn't know and be reminded of things you had long forgotten.

A young man in our community was killed in a car/train accident. The crossing gates didn't work and the two boys in the car never saw the train coming.

This kind of loss is devastating. The accident happened on Sunday evening. Many of the students of our small rural school didn't hear about the accident until they arrived at school. Students sobbed in the hallway. There were no words to comfort. The students helped each other. It was an awful time.

I was asked to do the funeral of this remarkable, vibrant young man from our community. He was a real character. He was one of the funniest and most playful people I've met.

Because of the gut-wrenching pain of this sudden loss, his mother requested that we not have any laughter in the service (she had been to some of my funerals and knew there was usually some laughing in the service). She felt this just wouldn't be appropriate. (In other words, the last thing she wanted to do was laugh).

I told her I believed forbidding laughter was a bad idea. I shared that the only way to remember her son was to remember who he was and the playful spirit that inhabited him. If we remembered him, we were going to laugh. I asked her to trust me. She did.

Because of the circumstances, the funeral service was held in the school gymnasium. This particular funeral was going to involve three different school districts. Two students were killed. They were from different school districts. The mother of my teen was a teacher in yet another school district. Consequently, hundreds of students were present. As it turned out close to 1000 people were in attendance.

The day after this young man died, when everyone at the school was finding out about the death, we wanted to give the students something concrete to do. (In these times you feel the need to do *something*). We asked students to write down their favorite memories of Dannen. Some of these were very funny, others were tender. All of them reminded us of the greatness of our loss as well as the blessing we experienced through his life.

It was one of the most difficult funerals I have ever done in my life. I didn't want to talk to anyone beforehand. My son was a classmate of this young man and his parents were my friends. I had to fight my own grief to do what needed to be done.

During the funeral we remembered Dannen

affectionately. There was laughter often followed by tears. We shared stories for a long time. It reminded us that Dannen had indeed lived and that he enriched our lives.

I asked the question everyone (including me) was asking, "Why?" We looked at the book of Job in the Bible. Job had horrible losses that came one right after another. He was a wonderfully faithful man and did not know why all this was happening.

Job's friends suggested that these horrible things must be a consequence for something Job was doing or not doing that was wrong. Some suggested he needed more faith. We know this wasn't the case from the first chapter of the book.

Job continued to plead his case before his insensitive and theologically challenged friends. He said he wished he could talk to God directly. He had some questions he would like God to answer. (Perhaps you have said something very similar).

At the end of the book of Job, the Lord made an appearance. He said to Job: "Before you ask me any questions I have a few questions for you." Most of those questions start with the words, "Where were you when . . ." It was a reminder that Job was trying to take the gracious Creator of the universe to task for His actions.

At the end of the questioning Job could only humbly sit before the Lord.

God never answered Job's questions. He knew Job could not understand what was going on in the spiritual world that was at this point beyond him. The message from Job is this: In the hard times when we have no answers, God simply says, "Trust Me." He asks us to trust His character and His love. He wants us to trust that the Creator of all the Earth will always do what is right; even if we don't understand what he is doing.

At the end of the funeral we all cried deeply. I was physically and emotionally exhausted. Many years after that day it still seems like yesterday.

Following the service at the luncheon held at a church, the mother came up to me. She said simply, "You were right. The humor was appropriate." She hugged me.

I wasn't looking for credit or affirmation. My goal was simply to remind this wonderful family that even though their son had died . . . he also lived and lived well.

A 19-year-old woman was murdered by a stranger crashing a New Year's Eve party at her home. The young people at the party were deeply traumatized as was the entire community.

Rebuilding Your Life After Grief and Loss

As I talked and mourned together with her parents I wrestled with what to say at this funeral. There was anger, there was profound sadness, and there were even various people blamed for what they did or didn't do.

I was convinced my job in the funeral was to remind people that we needed to remember Maddie not as the girl who was murdered. We needed to remember her as the vibrant young woman she was.

Once again, I told stories (many of them very funny). We wept, we laughed, we wept again. I reminded those who were in attendance that life is about choices. Hundreds of choices made differently may have resulted in a different outcome that night. But by the same token, choices (whether to turn to God or away from Him; whether to be filled with anger or with gratitude for Maddie's life; whether to blame or support each other) would determine how we coped in the future.

This is the challenge for you: work hard to remember and celebrate the fact that the person you loved lived. Their life may have been way too short. It may seem like they had so much more to give. However, in the sadness, remember that the reason for your grief is that this person touched your life. You grieve because you loved. This relationship was something special. Work hard to remember and celebrate why it was such a special relationship. Write down any positive memories and review them often. Choose to celebrate life rather than fixate on death.

Rebuilding Your Life After Grief and Loss

3
Special Circumstances

There are some unique losses that deserve special comment. These are situations that bring out *extreme* grief and emotion. There are more qualified people than me to talk about these subjects, but I can give you some introductory thoughts.

Multiple Losses

When several family members are killed in a car accident or many family members are killed in a "natural disaster" (like a tornado, hurricane, tsunami etc) or anytime there is a cluster of personal losses (like several losses in a relatively short period of time) grief becomes very difficult for the people who survive. You are reeling from one loss when the second one hits and seems to derail everything.

The difficulty here is that you are drowning in grief. It comes at you wave after wave and it is too much to absorb. The empty house, empty places at the dinner table and the deafening quiet are all overwhelming.

Experts say the only way to get through this time is to take the time to grieve each loss individually. For example, take one week to fully enter into the different areas of grief from the loss of your spouse. Then the next week you take time to grieve the loss of your child and so on until you have had the chance to grieve individually for each loss.

For example, you might take the loss of the first person and sit down and write down all the losses you have incurred through just this one death. Write down memories. You might even write a letter to this particular individual. It may seem crazy, but it is therapeutic to write down in words what is floating around in your head.

During the next week you start the process all over again but this time for another of person. We need to grieve each person individually so we can honor them in a way that brings healing. To try to grieve everyone at once feels like you are not really honoring or remembering anyone.

It is tempting at this point to feel God is being unfair. I cannot explain to you the work of the Lord. He tells us in Isaiah 55:9,

> For just as the heavens are higher than the earth,
>   so my ways are higher than your ways
>   and my thoughts higher than your thoughts.

Just because we don't understand the reason why something happened does not mean that there is no reason! God allows the things that happen for reasons that are beyond our ability to grasp. However, to push God aside when we need His comfort so desperately, is an over-reaction. It is like the old adage of "throwing the baby out with the bath water."

In this time of pounding loss, you need the strength, comfort, and healing that comes from the Lord alone. You would be well served by being part of the fellowship of a church family. You may need to "borrow" from the strength of some others during this time of devastation.

Suicide

My first experience with a suicide was with a successful businessman in our town. He was an active member in our church. That morning he put a can of coffee on the front seat of his truck along with his sandwich for lunch and then went out to his farm. He then took out his gun and ended his life.

I reeled from the suddenness of the loss as did the rest of our community. I was even more stunned when someone stopped me on the street to say they were praying for me because they knew it would be hard to do a funeral when I knew someone wasn't going to Heaven. I was dumbstruck.

This man I talked to grew up with the belief that suicide was the ultimate sin. If you took your life, there was no time to repent after you had done so. Therefore, you were lost.

This thinking is why people often try to cover up a suicide. They don't want people to know that their love one died in such an embarrassing and (they think) god-forsaken way. They often say they do not want the mention of suicide in the service (even though most people know exactly what happened).

As I was preparing the service for this man I admired and mourned. I came across this insightful quote from R.C. Sproul's book "Surprised by Suffering",

> I was once asked on a television talk show if people who committed suicide could go to heaven. I answered with a simple, "Yes." My answer caused the switchboard lights to glow like a Christmas tree. The host was shocked by my

response.

I explained that suicide is nowhere identified as an unforgivable sin. We do not know with any degree of certainty what is going through a person's mind at the moment of suicide. It is possible that suicide is an act of pure unbelief, a succumbing to total despair that indicates the absence of any faith in God. On the other hand, it may be the sign of temporary or prolonged mental illness. It may result from a sudden wave of severe depression. (Such depression can in some cases be brought on by organic causes or by unintentional use of certain medication.)

One psychiatrist remarked that the vast majority of people who commit suicide would not have done so had they waited twenty-four hours. Such an observation is conjecture, but it is conjecture based upon numerous interviews of persons who made serious attempts at suicide but failed and consequently recovered.

The point is that people commit suicide for a wide variety of reasons. The complexity of the thinking process of a person at the moment of suicide is known comprehensively by God. God takes all mitigating circumstances into account when he renders his judgment on any person.

> Though we must seek to discourage people from suicide, we leave those who have done it to the mercy of God.[2]

In preparing for the funeral for this man I asked the family for permission to address the issue directly. They graciously agreed that it would be foolish to deny what everyone was talking about.

When I started to speak about suicide the congregation seemed to lean forward to hear what I had to say. People were hungry to talk about this horrible experience of losing someone through suicide.

I drew a verbal picture: "Let's say I served the Lord and my community faithfully throughout my life. At the end of my life my health and mental state required I be placed in a Nursing Home to adequately care for my needs."

"While in the Nursing home I begin to suffer effects of dementia. I become combative and inappropriate in my language and my behavior. When I die would you conclude that I was excluded from

---

[2] R. C. Sproul, *Surprised by Suffering* (Wheaton, IL: Tyndale House Publishers, 1988), 181–182.

Heaven because of my behavior? "

"Most likely you would conclude that the dementia should not be counted against me anymore than the negative impact of a stroke should be a determining factor for someone else."

"I am arguing that it is the same with someone who took their own life. They may not have been in their right mind (who packs their lunch when they are planning to take life?) and therefore they are not held accountable for their actions."

I hope people left with a different perspective on suicide and God's response to suicide. Suicide is hard enough to handle without feeling that God has tossed your loved one aside.

When someone commits suicide there are some unique issues that have to be dealt with.

First there are the unanswered questions. Why did they do this (and often even a note does not make sense of the thinking process)? How could they leave this mess for us to deal with?

Second, you may feel guilty that you were not present or that you did not "recognize the signs." There is always that feeling that you could have stopped the death from happening. You may be tormented by questions such as, "What did I miss?" "Could I have stopped this?" "Did they hate me so much that they were trying to get away from me?"

It is hard enough to live our own lives. Trying to take responsibility for the lives of others is unrealistic and destructive. Most people who successfully commit suicide are actually at peace before the act. They make a decision (albeit a bad one) and they relax. We must accept the fact that some people are going to do things that are hurtful and we can't stop them.

Third, there is anger associated with suicide. It may seem strange but that anger is usually directed at the one who took their own life.

I was confronted with an attempted suicide once of someone close to me. I was surprised at how angry I was. I was angry that this person would choose to leave me in such a manner. I was angry that this person would have left me with a mess to clean up. I was angry that I was the one who would have had to face the crowds of people. I would be the one who had to live with the mess, the questions, and the guilt of all of it. I wanted to be sympathetic and to help this person, but I have to admit I was also angry.

Acts of Violence

It is very hard to deal with acts of senseless death: a drive-by shooting, a terrorist attack in a public place, a domestic abuse fatality, a hazing gone horribly bad, a senseless muder. It is hard to grieve in these situations because what happened is so sudden and it doesn't make sense.

Too often anger at the perpetrator becomes our focus. Sometimes grief does not actually begin until the legal issues are settled because all the focus is on gaining "justice."

It is important to grieve for this loss the same way you grieve the loss of others. To do so you may need to erect some boundaries and decide how much you will be involved in the criminal part of the process.

It is a good idea to elect a spokesman for the family to talk to reporters and lawyers. Try to isolate yourself from the drama of the legal parts of the drama. The many people clamoring for your time will stir up your anger and keep you from dealing with your loss.

Third, take your time. There may be lawyers, law-enforcement officials, and interested bystanders. You may even have news people looking for statements. Some of these people are just doing their job. However, you have a job also: you must grieve. If possible leave as much of these things as possible to others. Free yourself to deal with the horrible trauma you have faced. You will likely need special help to deal with this kind of loss.

In a sudden shocking loss such as this one of the hindrances is the outpouring of emotion from others. Sometimes the comfort of others can be like a drug that we need. Unfortunately, others go back to their normal life and you are still craving the comfort of others.

There will always be some who are drawn to the "excitement" that comes with a loss such as this. It is important not to let yourself get caught in that vacuum of emotion.

You will be dealing with two very different emotions: anger with a desire for justice, and the profound and seemingly unshakeable grief. You will have to keep working to see the difference between these two things. They are deeply intertwined but they are not the same thing.

This is a time when you need family members. You have to help each other in this time. The person who one day is strong to help you will need you to be strong from them at other times.

The sooner you can get routine back into your schedule the better. The nature of the loss is too overwhelming to just sit and ponder every day. You need some kind of distraction to help pull you through each day.

The Death of a Child

When a child dies the entire family is rocked. We all know that this is not the way the world was designed to function. Children are to bury their parents, not the other way around.

One of my first funerals was given to me at the very last minute. The Senior Pastor had walking pneumonia and could not do the funeral. He needed me to fill in. I walked in and was immediately troubled by the small casket at the front of the room. I talked to the funeral Directors and it turned out this little girl was savagely beaten to death by mom's boyfriend. The anger in the room was overwhelming.

Family members were angry at the man who did this (he was in jail), angry at the mother for getting mixed up with such a guy, and just plan angry at the situation. I don't remember anything I said that day.

The death of a child heightens emotions no matter how the child died. This is true for a child who was stillborn, one who died of Sudden Infant Death Syndrome (SIDS), Leukemia or other disease or even a car accident. Such a loss can put a huge strain on the family. Many couples have divorced after the death of a child because one spouse feels the other spouse is not grieving the way they think they should be grieving. This creates division and feelings that one of the parties is less caring than the other. Sometimes we blame when we are searching for answers. This only makes the grief harder.

When a child dies you will need someone to talk to. Take advantage of counselors. Go and visit with your Pastor or someone with a reputation for wise counsel. I must remind you again that people grieve differently. Just because one spouse is not grieving the same as another only means they are processing the grief differently.

Children Grieving

Let me add an aside here: How do you help a child grieve when someone they love dies? How much should a child be told about a loss. Here are some general suggestions:

1. Recognize that the child knows "something is going on." Face that fact and be honest. Tell the child as much truth as they can handle. If you are not willing to talk about the loss you will be teaching your children that people do not discuss loss.
2. Answer questions naturally. There will be questions children will ask that most adults would not ask (they might ask about the corpse, the

funeral, about the people talking to them at a visitation. They may ask what happens to a person when they die (see the last chapter of the book and the questions there) or what it feels like to die.) If you don't know an answer don't make one up! It is OK to not have answers and the sooner the children realize this, the better. It is fine to say, "I don't know."

3. Speak of death as a person of faith recognizing that death is a normal part of the process of life. In other words, use this death as a teachable moment. Use this time to teach a child about life after death, faith in Jesus, and the glories of Heaven. You can help a child begin to see death as a time of transition that we need not fear. Try to be accurate, in other words, don't say the person who died has now become an angel (there is nothing that indicates this is a fact), or that the person who died is still here among us. Let the child know that the person they loved is with Jesus and now is enjoying a new and wonderful life.

4. Speak carefully using words a child can understand. Saying "God took someone . . ." may make a child afraid that God is going to come and "take" them also. Even the idea of "falling asleep" can be scary to a child. It is best to say, "They

died" or "They went on to Heaven."
5. If a child wants to see the body, touch the person, or give them a kiss, let them. Explain that the body is made to look like it is still alive but it is not. By the same token, if the child does NOT want to see the body do not force them.

Everyone hopes we never have to face one of these horribly traumatic losses. However, it is best to be prepared.

Death and loss are a natural part of life. However, some of the circumstances of loss are difficult. However, everything else we said so far still applies: in the time of loss we must choose to remember and celebrate the fact that the person also LIVED.

Hopefully some of the suggestions in the next chapters will give you some very practical ways to re-purpose life to grow from even the most devastating of losses.

4

Getting Help

One of the barriers to healing from loss is our human tendency to feel we have to make it through things on our own and in our own strength. God made us as part of families, churches, and communities so we could help each other through times such as this.

Many churches and hospitals have grief support groups that can be a great help. If you have worked with Hospice (and even if you haven't) they are a great source of help even after someone has died. It is not a sign of weakness to ask for help. The road of grief is a road we all will travel. We need to help each other.

Let me focus for the rest of this book on things you can do that will be very helpful.

Refuse the Road of Denial

We spend a good deal of time pretending we are fine. We deny the facts, the pain, and sometimes we even deny the impact of the loss.

The energy you expend trying to maintain your charade will drain you and in time, will damage you emotionally. It will leave you feeling very alone and will delay your recovery.

Face what is happening to you. Instead of simply telling people you are fine, tell them the truth. Tell them you have good days and bad days. Most intuitive friends will ask, "Is this a good day or a bad day?"

When I see people who have recently had a loss I will ask them, "How are things going?" Often they say, "I'm fine." I make eye contact and simply say, "Really?" and many times these people will then break down.

I know, you don't want to burden people with your pain. But, this is what friends are for, to help you carry heavy burdens in life.

It is true that people sometimes say, "How are you?" but they don't really want to know. They are just being polite. I suggest if someone asks the question, tell them the truth. Assume they want to help you. If they really didn't want to know, they shouldn't have asked the question and I am pretty sure they won't make that mistake again!

You help other people to help you when you are honest. When everyone tells everyone else they are fine all the time, we believe there must be something wrong with us if we are not fine. It's OK to let people know grief hurts.

Tell Others What You Need

At a time of loss dozens of people will say, "If you need anything, let me know." I suggest you let them know what you need. Some people will respond poorly but there are those few who really will help you. And right now, you need them.

Here are some specific ways for people to help. If you don't tell people, most won't know they can help in such practical ways.

- "Please don't stop talking about the person I lost. Your memories may bring tears but that is not a bad thing. I am grateful for any memory you can share with me." One of the most painful parts of grief is the feeling that others have forgotten and you are alone in your grief. This is especially true of one who has been ill for a long time.
- "Could you stop by and visit regularly? I am so very lonely."

- "Would you help me work through some of the details of the estate? I am overwhelmed with all there is to do." There are belongings to sort through, payments to make, and sometimes there is even insurance money that needs to be invested. You may be unfamiliar with bills that need to be paid and how to make something work. Ask for help. People are eager to help if they know what you need them to do.
- "Can you find me help to rake leaves, cut my grass, or shovel snow? These are things I just don't have the energy to do."
- "Would you call me once in a while in the evening? Those times are so lonely for me."
- "Could we go out to eat once in a while? I hate eating alone."
- "Would you just sit quietly with me for a little while?"
- "Could you help me clean the house before all the family gets here?"

Many people want to help. They just don't know what to do. People make food because they don't know how else to express their sorrow. Give them options. Tell them how they can help. You can only eat so much food.

Make Time to Remember

It is important to take the time to sort through pictures and remember the good times you shared. It is valuable to talk with family and friends and to share the great stories of your life with the one who has passed.

These times of remembering help you to move from focusing on the loss, to remembering and giving thanks for the life. Yes, there will be tears (the good stories remind you of what you have lost). However, the stories also remind you of the blessing you enjoyed. It will help you to begin celebrating a life rather than mourning a death.

Strengthen your Faith

At the time of a death we ask ultimate questions. It is hard even for an atheist to stand at the graveside of someone they love. The notion that "this is all there is" is hard to accept. The meaninglessness of life seems stark as you stand before the remains of the person you loved.

The Bible (in Ecclesiastes) says it is better to go to a funeral than a place of feasting. The reason for this is that funerals force us to ask ultimate questions: "Is this all there is? What lies beyond the grave? What is the purpose of life?

Frankly, I don't know how anyone handles a death without some kind of belief system.

As for me, my Christian faith sustains me in the times of loss. I believe Jesus rose from the dead and promised that everyone who puts their trust and faith in Him will also rise.

I believe the notion of Judgment and Heaven and Hell make sense of life. Wrongs will be righted, good will be rewarded. Evil people will be judged.

Whenever grief begins to well up I remind myself of the death and resurrection of Jesus and recall that this shows me that this life is not all there is.

The Bible pictures life beyond the grave as a life that has been purged of sin, heartache, sadness and pain. Instead it is filled with wholeness, reunion, an an intimacy with the Lord that fills in all the gaps that we used to have in life.

If you have drifted from the church I encourage you to find a church that preaches the Bible and not pop psychology. If you can't find a good church immediately, I invite you to the website of the church where I serve: www.unionchurch.com.Check out our YouTube channel: "unionchurchLH." You can watch messages delivered on a wide variety of topics.

Rebuilding Your Life After Grief and Loss

Open your Bible. I encourage you to read in either the gospels (Matthew, Mark, Luke and John) or read through the Psalms. The Psalms are filled with emotions you will identify with. Watch carefully for how the Psalmist works through His emotions. The promises of God will give you an anchor that will hold strong in the most tempestuous times. (My book "Psalms of the Heart" can help you get started.)

Rebuilding Your Life After Grief and Loss

5
Re-purpose Difficult Days

Some days are harder to face than others after a loss. There are anniversaries (the anniversary of marriage, of the day of death, of the funeral, and even the anniversary of the day your loved one was first diagnosed), birthdays, holidays, and special days you celebrated as a family. These are hard times and you need to prepare for them.

Instead of dreading the day, make plans to re-purpose these painful days and difficult memories. In other words, deliberately work to remember the good things about the life of your loved one instead of simply re-living the pain. If you do this, these days can become welcome reminders of the way your life was blessed through the person you love rather than focusing on their departure.

My mother was really looking forward to turning

80. She wanted to have a party for her birthday in August. My sisters an I had already started to make plans for mom's party. She died suddenly in the February before her birthday.

As her birthday approached, we dreaded the day. Then we decided that we (her children and family) would get together to celebrate her birthday in her memory. We would celebrate Grace-Day (My mom's name is Grace)!

We all went to her favorite restaurant. We had a cake that was decorated just for her. We shared stories about mom. We laughed and we cried. My nieces had taken all of mom's old sweatshirts and cut them up to make blankets for my sisters and me. Others gave token gifts in memory of mom.

It was good to be together and to remember and grieve together. We only had one difficult experience. The waitress didn't understand what we were doing and (in trying to help) became very insistent on putting candles on the cake and placing the cake in front of the person who was celebrating the birthday. We tried to simply say 'that's not necessary' but she was undeterred. As a result, one of the priceless memories from that night was the look on her face when we told her that the guest of honor had died. My mom would have loved it! We will now tell that story every time we remember mom's birthday! We chose to turn the day into a celebration of life rather than a re-living of the pain of death.

Before my mom's house sold my sisters and nieces all went over to the house for one last meal at the house. It was an emotional time but an appropriate way to say goodbye.

A woman came to my office one-day asking for help. Her grandmother had died in the Nursing Home and she had to pass the Nursing Home every day several times when she went to work and went home for lunch. Every time she passed the home she started crying as she remembered the suffering of her Grandma. I suggested she change her thought process just slightly. Instead of remembering Grandma's death, why not remember something about her life, some positive memory, every time she passed the facility?

She told me a week later that this simple change of focus had helped wonderfully.

My Grandfather died and shortly after my aunt (his daughter) died suddenly on December 23rd. (It has been 35 years and I still remember that time vividly every year. The only difference is that now I welcome the chance to remember my aunt). On the 24th (the day she was pronounced dead) we went to her home and opened the gifts she had purchased. It was a devastating time. (I vividly remember that she bought me a pair of green corduroy pants that were kind of in style way back then. It was years before I could discard those pants because they were the last thing I had from my aunt.)

Lois was the aunt who had never married and she gave herself freely to all the nieces and nephews. She often invited us to do things with her. Once she took me bowling with my girlfriend at the time and kept me busy all day as a setup for a surprise 21st birthday. We all loved Lois, and it was a devastating blow when she died so suddenly.

One year later we gathered as an extended family for Christmas. Everybody was upbeat. No one acknowledged the "elephant in the room." When it came time for dinner, the family asked me to pray (sometimes as Pastors it feels like no one else can thank God, but I digress . . .). As I started the prayer I said, "Lord, we are very much aware of a couple of empty chairs at our table today."

As soon as I said those words I began to hear sniffles. I wondered if people would be angry that I made people cry. However, I knew we had to address the reality of our loss.

Following the dinner, I had several people who

took me aside, thanked me, and said astonishingly, "I thought I was the only one who was thinking about them." Everyone was so afraid of upsetting everyone else that it seemed that no one really cared! Nothing could have been further from the truth.

Once we acknowledged our sense of loss we could continue with our celebration. From that point on people shared memories and told stories about my grandfather and aunt. We laughed and we cried. We grew closer as a family as we remembered and grieved together.

One of the things you might do to remember is get out a copy of the funeral service (if you have it) or the picture slide show from the funeral. Take it/them out on the anniversary of the death and read through the remarks and watch the pictures once again. It is surprising how many things we forget.

I like to take out photographs and videos on these special times. I do this because I want to remember life, not death. Sure, I cry. It is because I miss this person that I loved. However, I would much rather remember than forget. After I remember I try to thank God for the blessings that filled my life because of the person I love.

Perhaps on that first Thanksgiving after the loss you could take a little time to go around the table and have everyone share one memory of the person who died. It may be emotional, but it will help you grieve and heal. It will also help young children appreciate the lives of the people that made such a huge investment in their lives. They will all benefit from hearing the stories. You will help them appreciate their heritage AND teach them how to grieve productively.

Before you get to Christmas why not ask family members to write down their favorite memories. Assemble all those memories and make copies for everyone in the family. Make sure everyone opens them at the same time. The celebration will stop for a little while as everyone pages through the book. Again there will be tears and laughter. You may need to remind people who are embarrassed by the tears that tears reveal that you cared and loved the person.

You can do the same thing with family pictures. It is easy to make photo books on the Internet. You can be as creative as you care to be. Your Christmas celebration will stop for a while as people look through the pictures. I guarantee that the most treasured gift will be those photos.

Perhaps you can give everyone something that belonged to the person who died. It is best if there are stories associated with each gift. I wear a tie clip that my dad used to wear every week. It isn't fancy but there is no amount of money you could give me for it. Little trinkets can become wonderfully precious if you take the time to think about appropriate gifts.

Use your imagination to prepare for special days. Have fun. Celebrate the life that was lived. Deliberately remember the blessings of that life. If you are creative and plan ahead, you can make these dreaded days into something special.

Too many times the trauma of death, or the slow process of dying, will overshadow the good memories. Don't let that happen! Don't let death overshadow the life that was lived.

You might be able to set up some "new holidays" (like our "Grace Day") in your family that will help you to remember. Remember that our tendency is to assume that we are the only one grieving. You are always wrong in that assumption. Talk, Remember, Celebrate.

Perhaps you can get together at a restaurant on the anniversary of the night your loved one died. That is a much better environment than sitting home alone rehashing all the painful details.

A good friend shared that an important mentor had died. It was a long slow death and they were not able to be at his side because he requested no visitors. His wife was well along with Alzheimer's which complicated things further. When Dave died all the guys he impacted came to the funeral. However, they were not able to grieve fully.

I suggested they all get together (inviting Dave's kids) and have a "Remember Dave night" they could go to a restaurant (somehow food seems to help) or meet in a home. The point of the evening would be to share memories and celebrate the life of this special person to them all.

It is only your imagination that will limit how you celebrate life. Do something fun. Laughter is a release of emotion just like tears are. Again, focus on remembering and giving thanks for life!!!

Pulling it all Together

The best way to face the difficult days (anniversaries, holidays and birthdays) is to plan ahead. Re-purpose those days. Create a way to use these days to remember and celebrate the life rather than rehash the death. Choose to focus on blessing rather than pain.

Besides, who doesn't enjoy a celebration?

6
Build on What You Are Learning

Loss is a learning experience. It changes the way you look at life and hopefully the way you look at death. Death becomes the necessary transition to the next and final destination in the journey of life. When we die, we graduate to the life God intended for us to live all along!

This of course doesn't mean you won't grieve. You will grieve. But it is helpful to realize that the grief is for your loss, and not the loss of the one who died.

Grief and loss are some of the most difficult classes we will take in life. But they are also life changing in what they can teach us. Pay attention at this time. There is much to learn.

You will find that this time can help you to appreciate life more than you did before. The reason this happens is because you now understand that life is temporary. You can't put off expressing your love and the feelings you have for others. We also can't put off enjoying life together.

Often after a death you find that survivors begin to travel, get involved in volunteer work, and start working on some of those projects we all save for "someday." Good for them! Death reminds us that "someday" may sneak up on us.

There will be things you wish had been said. Say those things.

There may be things you wish you had done with your children. Do them now.

There may be legal issues that you neglected to take care of: a will, advanced directives, or a power of attorney that need to be taken care of. Take care of those things now that you know how valuable they are.

You may need to think about your own arrangements for burial so your family doesn't have to guess at your wishes. It may have seemed morbid to think about such things before. Now you see that it is a loving act for your surviving family members.

You can and should build on the lessons you have learned through this experience.

Empathize More Intelligently

People who have been through a loss better understand what a grieving person may need. People sometimes say really dumb things and sometimes hurtful things at a time of loss.

I've heard people say things like this:
- The Lord must have needed another flower in His

Rebuilding Your Life After Grief and Loss

garden. (Why did He have to take mine?)
- Only the good die young. (That is not at all comforting . . . it is actually a little unnerving when you think about it.)
- They are in a better place. (That may be so but I am still here and I feel deserted).
- I know how you feel. (If you did know how I feel you wouldn't say such a thing. You would realize that each loss is different. You may empathize but you don't know how I feel.)

Now that you have been through a time of loss you know it is better to simply hug someone who is grieving. I often say, "I can't even imagine." Because you have experienced loss you now understand that what a person needs is for someone to share the pain with you.

What people need is not advice, they need someone willing to sit quietly and say nothing. Sometimes you need someone who will cry with you. You know there are no easy answers. There are no magic words. Your physical presence says more than any words could say.

The late Joe Bayly lost three of his children over the course of several years. In his book "The Last Thing we Talk About" shares his honest feelings.

> I was sitting, torn by grief. Someone came and talked to me of God's dealings, of why it happened, of hope beyond the grave. He talked constantly. He said

things I knew were true.

I was unmoved, except to wish he'd go away. He finally did.

Another came and sat beside me. He didn't talk He didn't ask me leading questions. He just sat beside me for and hour and more, listened when I said something, answered briefly, prayed simply, left.

I was moved. I was comforted. I hated to see him go.

You understand this don't you? You now know that personal presence trumps an unwanted answer every single time. You now have a new way to minister to others because you have been through the difficult classroom called loss. You don't have to have answers; you just need to be present.

You also understand that what you often need more than anything else at the time of loss are lots of practical things. You can lend an intelligent hand by doing practical things for the person.

- Come to the house and help clean.
- Help make phone calls.
- Put away food that people bring.
- Replant flowers.
- Call regularly over the next several months just to check in.
- Invite the survivor to dinner or go shopping with you.
- Send regular cards and notes.

- One woman I know used to crochet little blankets. She prayed over the blanket as she made it. She prayed for the person who would receive it. She gave lots of these "prayer shawls" away and I am sure they are all cherished.
- Offer to sit with someone in church. That first time back into church alone is hard. You feel like everyone is looking at you.
- Share some of what you have learned about practical matters. You must be careful here however. There is a natural tendency to start talking about your loss. The things you should share should be practical things. They may have to do with Social Security, collecting insurance monies, estate issues and more. You have been through this maze of headaches already and your experience can help minimize the headache to someone else. If the person wants to compare losses they will ask you for details.

Turn Your Attention to Those Who Remain

I know a woman who experienced a great trauma. A beloved member of the family died suddenly in a freak accident. Everyone (including me) was devastated by the loss. But no one took it harder than the grandmother.

Grandma could not stop crying. All she could talk about was the person who had died. She went out to his grave several times a day . . . for YEARS.

As a result, the rest of her family started to pull away.

They needed and wanted to keep living. Every time they saw this woman she pulled them back into a paralyzing grief. And if they were not willing to go back to that intense initial grief they were charged with not caring. Those words wounded family members.

The woman built a little shrine in her house. This kept people from wanting to come into the house. Other family members concluded they apparently were not important. They were wounded. They felt they not only lost their cousin – they also lost their Grandmother.

After a death we have to work hard to make existing relationships better. We can't bring the person who died back to life. We can however work hard to make memories with family members who remain.

Don't let your sadness provoke additional losses. Grieve, but then give attention to places where your attention can make a difference.

The person you loved died. But you didn't.

7
Building Memories While You Can

I have conducted over 300 funerals over the years. Each one is different.

In preparing for the funeral I like to sit down with a family and ask questions about the person who died (even when I knew them well). I want to get the family talking and sharing their stories. (This is therapeutic for the family and it gives me precious insights into the one who died). I listen carefully and take copious notes.

Every time I leave a home I feel there was so much more about this person that I wish I could have known.

When family members gather to talk about the one who has died they don't talk affectionately about how much money they made or the hours they worked. The things family members cherish are the little things: special moments, family traditions, and the things that made this person unique and cherished.

When you are laying on your bed knowing death is near, you will not wish you had spent more hours at work. No one is going to wish they had more possessions. What you will long for is more time to make memories. You will regret (and probably already do) that you did not spend more time with the people that you love.

With that in mind, let's talk about how you can make some special memories.

Ideas for Making Memories

One family sat around the table with me and they found that their dad had filled in one of those memory books (in this case it was more like a daily calendar). Such books have questions in them about your history and your job is to answer them. They relate to your childhood, your interests, your dating life, your hobbies, and what your childhood home was like.

One of the family members made copies of these pages for all of the 10 kids (and me). We spent a long time reading through the questions and answers. There was laughter and there was astonishment at things family members did not know. Some provoked stories of special times. This will always be a treasured possession for this family.

Right after this funeral I purchased a Mother's memory book for my mom. She faithfully filled out the pages and returned it to me. When she died I found memories of things I didn't know about. When I went back to this book, mom had explained it all in those pages. It is a wonderful keepsake.

(As an aside, my children purchased one of those books for me. I have been working on completing it for going on 8 years! But . . . I will finish because I know how valuable it is.)

Another woman was asked by a family member if he would video tape an interview with her. She agreed. She simply sat on her couch and talked about her life. Gladys talked about her upbringing, her life with her husband, her hobbies and so much more. When she died they asked if I would like to see the video. It was wonderful. It was a great idea. Perhaps you will want to interview various members of the family while you can still do so.

Work hard to create special events. Families remember trips that were taken and special times they shared. It doesn't really matter the destination of the trip. It is making the journey together that will be remembered forever. If you can afford it, take the family on a nice vacation. Go camping. Maybe you can just spend the weekend at a nearby hotel. Make a memory!

I love it when families take old movies, slides, or videos and put them on DVD. These are priceless memories that are now preserved and accessible.

My wife and I love answering questions. These are just miscellaneous questions that help you get to know each other. We have answered thousands of questions and never tire of getting to know each other better. I am working to do this with the entire family at our Sunday family gatherings. Children of every age can answer the questions and oh the things you will learn! I want to be intentional about sharing in the lives of those around me.

Develop special holiday traditions. Over the last few years I have had the Grand-kids cook for our Christmas meal. We make potato chip chicken and buffalo chicken. We have a great time together and everyone enjoys the meal that much more! It is my hope that someday when my family is talking about my life, they will talk about Christmas dinner cooking with Grandpa!

When my son turned 16 I decided that I needed to write him a letter for his birthday. I wanted to make sure that he knew how much I loved him and respected the man he was becoming.

That first letter began with the words, "I

remember the day you were born." To be honest it was an emotionally draining experience. It was so emotional to write the letter I could not give it to him or watch as he read it. I put it on the table so he would find it when he ate his breakfast. I was told that he cried when he read it.

The fact that he cried concerned me. Did he not know that this is how I felt about him or was it just nice to hear these things? It has been 16 years since I wrote that letter and I have written him a letter every birthday since then.

When my daughter's birthday came along I wrote (and continue to write) her a letter also. I also write one to my wife. I have added letters to my Grandchildren and my son and daughter–in-law. In each letter I try to express my heart. I share the wonderful traits that I see and the potential I believe God has placed in them.

Now as people open their birthday gifts they open the card that has the letter. Usually they will slide the letter into their pocket so they can read it in private.

One of the kids (I don't remember which one) received a letter their first birthday when they were away from home. They told their mom they were so glad to get the letter. They were afraid I was going to stop writing them.

I hope they have shoe boxes or files someplace where this stack of letters resides. And I hope that someday after I have gone to be with the Lord, that they will take out those letters and remember how much I loved them.

It takes time to write. People don't do much of that anymore. And that makes these notes, I hope, an even greater treasure.

As an aside, the birthday after my wife left me I did not want to celebrate my birthday. I was not in a celebratory mood. And my son (who works with me in ministry) handed me a card. Inside was a letter he wrote to me. It was the best birthday present I have ever received.

I heard about a parent who knew they were dying and would miss many of the significant days in the life of their child. So, this forward-thinking person wrote a letter to be given to their child at their baptism, their wedding, their graduation etc. What a wonderful idea and a cherished gift to these family members.

Perhaps you may want to buy gifts each Christmas that are unique and memorable. Maybe you want to buy a different book that has made an impact on your life for people every year. Or maybe you could make that gift a framed picture, a significant Christmas ornament, or a little do-dad that is significant only to the two of you. If you do this each year it will be something that person will cherish and will look forward to receiving. And someday I can envision them showing their Pastor all the things their mom or dad or sibling gave to them.

I hope you get the point. We aren't talking about spending money. We are talking about making memories. Personal memories.

Here's a question to get you started: How do you want to be remembered? What do you hope your family will say about you? What memories do you hope they will cherish? What lessons do you hope they will attribute to you?

You have time to be intentional about making these memories. But the time to start is now.

When the person you loved died, people shared (I hope) lots of memories. Pay attention to the things people remembered. Make sure that your family remembers you and the relationship you had together well.

Now, instead of moping around about your loss. Start working on making some memories that will be cherished in the future.

Rebuilding Your Life After Grief and Loss

8
Pay a Dividend

After we have lost someone that we love we may feel guilty if we start enjoying life again. It feels like we aren't showing respect. It is difficult for someone to think about remarriage after their spouse has died because they feel like they are being unfaithful.

We feel guilty if we laugh. We feel guilty if we have moments when we seem to forget that the person has died. We might even say, "I'm a horrible person."

Life will never be the same again, but that doesn't mean life is over! In fact, I would contend the worst thing you could do would be to stop living and spend too much time grieving.

Let me draw you a picture. I have served as Pastor of the church I serve for 35 years (as of this writing). I have in essence given my life to these people. I have walked with them through heartache and shared their joy at accomplishments and special events (births, weddings, graduations, promotions, etc.).

Let's say I finish preaching one Sunday and on the way home I am killed in a car accident (which would be really a freak accident since I live across the street from the church . . . but I digress).

If that happened I would hope that people wouldn't walk into the church building the next day as if nothing happened. If my son walked into my office the next day and said, "Good, he's finally gone and I can get the big office!" I would be quite disappointed.

I would want people to be sad. And so would you. I would hope the entire community would feel a sense of sadness that the "Community's Pastor" had died. It would be nice if people stood around and shared memories. It would be gratifying if the funeral was attended well. I want people to miss me when I am gone! You want that too.

However, here's the thing – you want them to grieve only for a season. I don't want the church to close or for my son to keep my office as a shrine. I want these people to pay dividends on the investment I made in them and in the church throughout my life.

In other words, I would want my son to be a better Pastor than his dad. I would want the people to live out those things they learned from me. I would want my children and grandchildren to build strong families that impacted many. My legacy will be carried on by those who remain.

Your loved one invested in your life. They wanted you to be what God created you to be. They worked hard to help you grow and to support you. They would certainly want you to miss them . . . but they wouldn't want you to stop living!

Do you remember the wonderful Richard Dreyfus movie, "Mr. Holland's Opus"? Mr. Holland was a musician, but times were tough and he had to take a job as a music teacher in an area high school. He had to learn how to teach students to love music.

Over his decades of teaching we are introduced to a bunch of different students. Many of them were profoundly impacted by Mr. Holland.

Mr. Holland however, never gave up his dream of writing a symphony. He felt his life was in a holding pattern and at times it was extremely frustrating.

Mr. Holland eventually became the victim of budget cuts. As he was leaving the school for the last time he heard a commotion in the auditorium. He opened the door to see what was going on and the auditorium was filled with his former students. They had come to commend him for a life well lived.

The key line of the movie was this, "Mr. Holland, we understand you were always working on writing a symphony that was going to make you famous. Mr. Holland WE are your symphony."

You are the music that remains from the life that has now passed. Your friend or family member spent a life time working on this symphony that is now in you. Don't pack it up! Play it! Live it! Make sure the life of your loved one pays wonderful dividends.

Do not feel guilty for moving forward with your life. For moving forward is what these people would want. That is what you would want too.

9
Nagging Questions

Sometimes we are haunted by questions. In this chapter I want to address (not always "answer") some common questions.

How can I be sure I am going to survive this heartache? For a while you may feel like life will never be the same again. And it won't be. But that doesn't mean life won't be good. If you do some of the re-purposing that I suggest in this book you will find that you begin to see the joy of living once again.

You will never forget the person who died. You will always ache from the loss. But you will also reach a point where you move forward in the "new normal" that is now your life.

Don't be afraid to get help. You may talk to professionals or even a Pastor or trusted friend. The journey of grief is easier to make if you don't have to make the journey on your own.

How do we know that there is really a life beyond the grave? I am not going to get into the proofs for the existence of God or try to defeat the arguments of atheists. There are lots of books devoted to just that subject.

The easiest answer to the question is that we know there is life beyond the grave because Jesus rose from the dead and told us it is so!

I believe it is a good thing to examine carefully the Resurrection of Jesus. One of my favorite books growing up was a book written by Frank Morrison called "Who Moved the Stone." Morrison was an attorney who originally set out to prove the Resurrection of Jesus was nonsense. He became a believer and wrote this book instead.

Lee Strobel was a reporter for the Chicago Tribune. His wife became a follower of Jesus and Strobel set out to "investigate" Jesus. He was sure the evidence would show that the story of Jesus was just an overblown myth. He became a follower of Christ and his book "The Case for Christ" has helped hundreds of thousands come to faith in Christ.

A quick rundown on some of the compelling evidence for the Resurrection of Jesus:

1. Jesus was definitely dead. The Romans were excellent executioners. Jesus had been beaten for many hours before his crucifixion. To make sure he was dead they pierced His side and the eyewitness testimony says water and blood came out. This would indicate the heart and the pericardium was pierced. Jesus did not pass out. He was not in a coma. He was dead.
2. Eyewitnesses. After His death and Resurrection, Jesus was seen several times and once it was by over 500 people.
3. An empty tomb. In fact the tomb (which had been guarded and sealed) still contained the grave clothes of Jesus . . . He just wasn't in them! The Jewish leaders and Romans would have gone to great lengths to find the body which they said was stolen. The Resurrection of Jesus made them all look bad. They had the power and the resources to find a stolen body. They came up with nothing.
4. A dramatic change in the disciples. These eleven men had all deserted Jesus. They were hiding because they believed they would be the next to die. Suddenly they were out in the temple courts with incredible courage and completely unafraid of death. They preached in the Temple area! Each

one of these men (except John) died as a martyr. Even under great duress not one of these men said it was all a lie. So either these men died for a lie or . . . they really did see Jesus!
5. There is NO evidence that the Resurrection did not happen (and lots that it did). There are many theories and alternate explanations of the facts but there is NO evidence.
6. There are personal encounters that seem to assure us that the Lord really is out there. Sometimes you just KNOW that the Lord is communicating with you.

Any time I begin to doubt in my faith I return to the evidence for the Resurrection. It is a powerful reminder that we are living now to live again. I find it easier to trust someone who has already been there and risen again.

If you have never examined the evidence don't draw conclusions until you do. You can start with one of the two books mentioned above. There are many more.

How do I know if my loved one is in Heaven? I can't bear the thought that they might not be there. The Bible tells us that there is only one way to

Rebuilding Your Life After Grief and Loss

Heaven, that is through genuine faith and trust in Jesus Christ as the only One who can save us.

This is not the same as going to church or being baptized or being confirmed. People can be religious, they can even feel "good" about Jesus, but still not trust Him.

To trust Jesus means to bet your life on Jesus. It means living as if He is the only One who can save you (which is exactly what He is). It means we try to follow Him trusting that He has done what is necessary for us to go to Heaven and live forever.

Only God knows the human heart. Only He knows if faith is genuine or superficial. Only He knows if someone is trusting or is only saying they are trusting Christ.

In the same vein, only God knows what is going on inside of someone before they die. I will never say that someone is going to Hell. That is not my call, it is the Lord's.

I had an experience with a man who at one time professed faith and then left his family and basically drank himself to death. I sat by his bedside, my back against the wall. He was struggling to breathe.

Suddenly he grabbed the railing in front of me and pulled himself onto his side. I thought he was going to say something to me. His eyes were wide open but he was looking above and past me. He was quiet as if he was listening to something (or someone). Then he lay back flat, relaxed and was gone.

I will always believe the Lord was talking to my friend Kyle and told him it was time to stop fighting, and come home.

Will we know each other in Heaven? I believe we will know each other. At the Mount of Transfiguration, the disciples somehow recognized Moses and Elijah. The Disciples knew it was Jesus who was talking to them. There will be a wonderful reunion in Heaven of those who are children of God through Christ.

Will I be married to my spouse in Heaven? What happens if I get re-married? Jesus said

> [30] For when the dead rise, they will neither marry nor be given in marriage. In this respect they will be like the angels in heaven. (Matthew 22:30)

There will not be marriage or weddings in Heaven. Some people are disappointed by this truth (others are relieved). However, Jesus wasn't teaching that loving relationships would not exist. He is teaching us that

EVERY relationship in Heaven will be deeper and richer than marriage was on earth. In other words, we won't need to get married to know true intimacy. Marriage will be replaced by something better.

What Happens to Us at the Moment of Death? Of course, until we actually die, we won't know what exactly happens at the moment of death. Here is what I think the Bible says will happen.

First, I believe we are met by Jesus. In John 14:3 Jesus said He is preparing a place for us and when everything is ready He will come and bring us to this place He has prepared for us.

Isn't that a comforting picture? We go from the hands of our family immediately into the arms of Jesus. What a wonderful picture that is. I like to think that just before the follower of Christ dies they hear someone call their name and discover that it is their Lord. I can hear Him say, "It's time to go home!" and then we feel His hand in ours and we step over the threshold.

Second, we are purified. As one man has expressed it:

> Here, responsibilities, pain and temptation. Here, harassment by the demonic, persecution by the

world, disappointment in friends. Here, relentless, remorseless pressure, requiring us to live at the limits of our resources and at the very edge of endurance. But there, rest: "the battle's o'er, the victory won." The turmoil is behind us and the danger passed. No more of the burden of unfinished work or the frustration of in-built limitations. No sin to mortify. No self to crucify. No pain to face. No enemy to fear.[3]

It is at this point that we will finally and fully be freed from sin and the desire to sin.

Third, we will be with Christ. Jesus told the thief on the cross TODAY (not tomorrow or the next day) you will be with me in paradise. In Philippians 1:22-23 Paul said,

> [21] For to me, living means living for Christ, and dying is even better. [22] But if I live, I can do more fruitful work for Christ. So I really don't know which is better. [23] I'm torn between two desires: *I long to go and be with Christ*, which would be far

---

[3] Quoted in Albert N. Martin Grieving, Hope, and Solace When a Loved One Dies in Christ. (Crucifom Press) chapter 6.

better for me.
                                    -Philippians 1:21-23

The minute we die we move to the presence of the Lord who died for us and whom we have longed to meet personally! Paul's argument is that it is better to go and be with the Lord but he believes the Lord wants him to remain and continue to minister. If we do not go immediately to be with the Lord and don't meet Him until the Lord returns, then the argument doesn't make any sense. There would be no advantage to dying now versus later.

Fourth, it will be time of fellowship with other believers and reunion with those whom we love and who have gone before us.

> [16] For the Lord himself will come down from heaven with a commanding shout, with the voice of the archangel, and with the trumpet call of God. First, the believers who have died will rise from their graves. [17] Then, together with them, we who are still alive and remain on the earth will be caught up in the clouds to meet the Lord in the air. Then we will be with the Lord forever.
>   -1 Thessalonians 4:16-17

Notice how the believers are all together. It is good to be reminded that these are the purified saints of God. Al Martin again describes the scene,

> They have been completely conformed to the moral image of Christ and endowed with every grace of Christ-like moral character, they all perfectly love their neighbors as they love themselves. No words are misunderstood, no motives are questions, different capacities and ability provoke no envy or jealousy but only add praise to God for the richness of God's gifts and graces perceived in one another.[4]

All those people we have missed will be there in the greatest reunion of all time. We will be reunited with those who impacted us in our spiritual life. We will also see the many who are in Heaven because God used us in some way. Imagine how humbling it will be to know that you were used of God to lead others to Him.

What if all my friends are in Hell?

Sometimes you will hear someone foolishly say,

---

[4] ibid

"Why would I want to go to Heaven if all my friends are in Hell?" The problem with this thinking is that Hell will be the place where the blessing of God has been removed. People in Hell are those who have rejected Christ and therefore they will live apart from Him and His gifts.

The thing is, people don't think about what it means that God's blessing is removed. Friendship, love, enjoyment, laughter . . . are all blessings from God! They will not be there in Hell. Your friends may all be in Hell (a very sad state of affairs you should be trying to rectify) but they will not be your "friends" in Hell. There will not be any parties, only agony. Those you called your friends will now be people who are just trying to survive.

Is my loved one still with me? I feel their presence.

There is no evidence in the Bible that our loved ones become angels or watch over us. This is a comforting thought, but I don't see any evidence it is the case.

It is possible the Lord is giving a special touch of His comfort by stimulating a memory that brings back a vivid feeling. There is no reason to think that your loved one is actually walking with you.

Heaven will be such a glorious place that is so far

superior to earth that I believe we will be completely absorbed in the presence of Jesus and the reunion of saints. I don't think people will be sitting around watching what we are doing on earth.

Is it a sin to be cremated?

This is a common question. There is no definitive answer in the Bible. The idea behind being buried (with our heads all toward the west so we can rise facing the eastern sky when Jesus returns) is to be ready for the resurrection.

However, we are going to get new and corrected bodies. The sinful body will give way to a spiritual body. God created us from dust once. I don't see why He won't do it again. Eventually, even the person in the casket will eventually decay to dust. It is possible that cremation is simply speeding up the process.

Cremation is a personal choice. Some people do it to lessen the cost. Others are thinking about ecology. In my mind as long as people are believers in Christ, it doesn't make a difference.

What if I don't want to have a funeral?

There is nothing wrong with not wanting a funeral (and the expense that comes with it). But please remember that the funeral is not for you, it is for those who remain. This is the place where people gather to share their stories and to celebrate your life.

A funeral service also gives the opportunity to share the message of the gospel with family and friends. In other words, it is a chance to honor the Lord of life.

The bottom line is that there is no Biblical injunction as to what you must do. It is not a sin to not have a funeral. However, it is important to think about others at this time.

What if I still have unresolved issues with the person who died?

There are times when someone dies more suddenly than we expected, and as a result, we are not able to say things we needed to say, or resolve the issues that needed to be addressed. This could be a confrontation (because of abusive behavior in the past, or a revelation that came after death), it could be an apology that needed to be extended, or love that needed to be expressed. What do you do?

First, you must realize that you will not be able to resolve these issues face to face. There will be questions that will never have answers. Words that can never be spoken. The desired explanations are buried with the one who has died. You must work to accept this truth.

Second, you may be able to talk to a family member and say what you need to say or ask the questions for which you would like answers. This may help resolve some of your discomfort.

It is important that you are very sensitive here. Your desire for resolution of your issues does not give you the right to be mean. Be sensitive to the fact that the people you want to talk to are also grieving. They are not the problem! Do not add to their pain. It may be better to talk to a counselor or Pastor.

Third, write a letter to the person who died. Take your time and think it through. If you are angry, write down why you are angry. If there are words that needed to be expressed, express them. If there are questions, ask them. Probe deep to reach the depth of your emotion.

Let me give you an example. Suppose the person who died abused you. In your letter you might tell the person that they stole your innocence, security, and any hope of a happy childhood. Explain how this trauma impacted the rest of your life. Write it all down. The goal is to be very specific about how you feel and why. What you are trying to do is understand *your own* emotions. Emotions are hard to address if you don't understand the source of those emotions.

When you are sure you have said what needed to be said, destroy the letter.

Some people are more comfortable going to the cemetery and talking to the headstone of the one who died. It is not that the person who died is listening. The person you need to have listening is You! Let me say it again, you are working to understand why *you feel* the way you do as specifically as possible.

Finally, give these issues to the Lord. We know the Lord of all the Earth will do what is right. Ask God to help you forgive. You may need to forgive the other person, or you may need (after confession and repentance) to forgive yourself. You can be honest with the Lord. Ask Him to help you heal and to learn from the pain. Trust him to right the wrongs.

Rebuilding Your Life After Grief and Loss

10
Concluding Thoughts

I hope you have found some encouragement and suggestions that will help you celebrate life even as you grieve your loss. Grief is a necessary part of life. Loving someone carries with it the risk (and reality) of loss. You can't have one without the other.

When loss takes over our lives we must work hard to remember that our loved one did not only die . . . they also lived. They blessed us, enriched us, and poured a part of themselves into our lives. This fact should be remembered and celebrated.

I have written these words as a follower of Jesus. I am a Christian Pastor and I believe the message of Christ changes the whole discussion of grief. Death is no longer an ending, it is a transition; a graduation; or a promotion. It is painful to those who are left behind but it is a supremely good thing for those who die "in the Lord."

Allow me to share a picture that has been very helpful to me.

Imagine two airports. At one you are standing at the departure gate. You are surrounded by loved ones who don't want to see you leave. There are tears. There are hugs that won't disengage and a pale of sadness hanging over the group as you head to the gate.

Now journey with me to the arrival gate. What a different picture we find there! People are jumping up and down with excitement. They watch out the window in anticipation of the arrival of their friend and family member. Tears of sadness are replaced with tears of joy. Sadness is replaced with smiles and laughter. The hugs given are joyful. There is a sense of celebration in the air.

Right now you and I are at the departure gate. Our loved one has left us, and we are sad. Someday it will be our turn to come out of the arrival gate. Our perspective will be different. The welcome will be warm. The sadness will be swallowed by joy.

It is tough to drive home from the departure gate.

My wife and I do a great deal of commuting. Every time we part company there is sadness. We are able to handle the times of separation because we look forward to the next time we will be together. The hope of the future tempers the sadness of the present.

It is important to remember that for every departure gate there is also an arrival gate.

Imagine another picture. You are near a creek and you hear the joyful sounds of children playing. As you approach you see a pile of clothes that have been discarded. You can imagine these children rushing to take off their clothes to enter the joys of the water.

As you look out on the children you see that they are having a great time. They don't have a care in the world!

Turn around with me and go back to the pile of clothes. When you see the oine you love in a casket all you are seeing is their "pile of clothes." The person you cherish has discarded their worn-out body, so they can joyfully embrace the new life that comes as a follower of Jesus.

It is my hope and prayer that these thoughts will bring you comfort and strength in your time of grief.

Rebuilding Your Life After Grief and Loss

11
To the Reader

To the reader who is not a Christian . . . throughout the course of this book I have approached things from the perspective of one who believes there is life beyond the grave because of the work of Jesus. I hope your experience of grief has led you to think further about what happens after we die.

There are many theories of course. Some say we are recycled (reincarnated). Others say we become "one with the universe" (but frankly I have no idea what that means). And a growing number believe death is the end of our existence. We live, we die, and that is all there is.

This last view (the atheist view) sees life as a mad rush to nowhere. As a result, little in life really matters. You can do whatever you want as long as you don't get caught by someone who doesn't want you doing what you are doing. Nothing matters.

I believe this kind of view makes grief all the

more terrible. There is no hope.

The message of the Christian faith is that God created us for a purpose. He wanted us to know Him and to enjoy a life in relationship with Him. However, we took the freedom God gave us to rebel against the very one who made us. We rebelled against authority of all kinds but especially against Him.

The Old Testament is the story of the beginning of God's rescue plan. God chose one man, Abraham, and decided he would use him to reveal His love for mankind. He decided to save the world through one of the descendants of Abraham. God told Abraham exactly what He was going to do. He was going to work through one nation: Israel.

The Bible tells us that God did not choose Israel because they were better than everyone else. He chose Israel because when the world saw what God would do (and continues to do) through this tiny nation, they would have to conclude the God of Israel is the true God.

The Jewish people were given the Ten Commandments and an extensive moral code that was designed to point humanity in the direction God created us to travel. But rebellion continued.

When King David came to the throne the talk became quite specific about a Messiah (a Savior) who would come into the world to erase the barrier between mankind and what God called "sin."

As we skip ahead after hundreds of prophecies about this Messiah, a Jewish man by the name of Jesus was born in a remarkable way. It was a simple birth; a humble birth; but a birth that fulfilled all the prophecies of a coming Messiah.

This one man lived the way God told us to live. He spoke with an authority that captivated people and had a supernatural power. He performed miracles that confounded the masses. He brought people back from the dead at least twice (that we know of). He caused blind people to see, deaf people to hear, paralyzed people to walk. He even walked on water one memorable night on the Sea of Galilee. But He did not fit in with the status quo. The Jewish leaders hated Him.

You probably know the story. These leaders had Jesus arrested on trumped up charges. They blackmailed the Roman governor who had Jesus crucified.

The talk of Jesus as the One who would save us seemed hollow and empty. All His talk about believing in Him and living after we die seemed a fantasy.

The Jewish leaders had a little more faith than his

own disciples. They remembered that Jesus talked about rising from the dead. While the disciples hid, afraid that they would be arrested and killed, the Jewish leaders had the tomb of Jesus sealed and soldiers stand guard. There was no way they were going to let anyone claim that Jesus rose from the dead.

But then on the third day the tomb was empty. The soldiers told a lame story about the cowering disciples coming to steal the body. (If that had been true the soldiers would have been executed for letting it happen).

Soon people started to say they had seen Jesus. Over 500 people said they saw Him and talked with Him. The evidence for the Resurrection is quite compelling (see page 83-84) for more on the Resurrection).

Jesus (and then His followers) said that the person who believes Jesus was from God and gave His life to rescue us; the person who believes with all their heart that Jesus can give us life beyond the grave; will live even though they die.

The person who is willing to "bet their life on Jesus" is a true believer (merely going to church does not make you a believer).

So, to you, my hurting friend, I invite you to

welcome Jesus. He loves you. And even though you may not understand the what and why of what has happened in your life, I urge you not to turn away from the One who gives hope in the midst of tragedy and loss. He is the One who gives you strength. He is the One who brings light in the darkness and meaning to what seems meaningless. I urge you to turn to Him not only because it is comforting (and it is!), but because it is *true*, and will change you in ways that enrich your life.

Right now you can talk to the Lord. Tell Him that you want the salvation and new life that He offers. Confess your heartache and lean fully on Him. Then pick up your Bible and get to know the One who knows you better than you know yourself. He is what you have been looking for. He is the One you need.

To the Christian

My fellow brother or sister, there is nothing sinful about grieving. There is no shame in tears. The ache of loss does not need to be denied or hidden. Grief does not show a lack of faith. It is a process that we all must work through.

First, let me encourage you once again to let others help you. Be honest about your needs. Turn to your brothers and sisters in Christ. There is no need to pretend to "have it all together." God made us to help each other.

Second, I encourage you to build depth in your faith during this time. Dig deeper into the Lord. Read His Word. Be honest with God in prayer. More than ever before, you must stop pretending. Cling to the truth of the Resurrection of Christ. Believe His promises to you.

There will be times when you read the Bible and you feel like you received absolutely nothing. Keep reading. Around the next page may be that life-altering insight that changes your life. At times, prayer will seem empty. Confess your lack of desire to pray. Tell God the truth, that you just don't feel like talking now. Tell Him that you are willing to just listen. Ask Him to speak.

Finally, celebrate life. Celebrate the life of the person you loved. Celebrate their blessing in your life. Celebrate because you, of all people, understand that when this life ends, another that is greater begins.

Continue to be faithful to the One who is always faithful to you.

Please take the time to share your review of this book on Amazon.com (especially if you found it helpful).

Acknowledgements

I want to thank the McDonough District Hospital Hospice Department. Most of what is in these pages was "tested" at the yearly Hospice Service of Remembrance. The encouragement and kindness of the Hospice workers inspired this book.

A huge thanks to Rick Goettsche, Ruth Swan, Michael and Donna Lawrence, Karen Moore, and my wife Debbie for taking the time to proofread all or parts of this book. It is a better book because of your suggestions.

Rebuilding Your Life After Grief and Loss

Other books by Bruce Goettsche

Faith Lessons: Lessons in Faith from Genesis

Lessons in the Wilderness (Exodus-Deuteronomy)

Finding Your Way Through the Fog (Colossians)

Joy: Finding it, Keeping it (Philippians)

Difficult People: Dealing with Those Who Drive You Crazy (with Rick Goettsche)

Songs of the Heart (Psalms)

A Christian Handbook to Surviving Divorce

Meeting with God (a one year devotional)

Rebuilding Your Life After Grief and Loss

Meeting with God Year 2

Meeting with God Year 3

All of these book are available in print and kindle formats from Amazon.com

Rebuilding Your Life After Grief and Loss

About the Author

Bruce Goettsche is the Pastor of the Union Church of La Harpe Illinois where he has served since 1982. He graduated from Trinity International University in Deerfield Il with a BA in Biblical Studies. He earned his Masters in Christian Education and a Master of Divinity degrees from Northern Baptist Seminary.

Bruce is married (Debbie) and has two children. His son, Rick serves with him in ministry. His daughter Rachel is a physical therapist. He also has two step-sons (Zeko and Derek). He has several grandchildren as of this writing.

Bruce loves to write and is heard on a local radio broadcast, "God's Truth for Daily Living."

You can contact him at bruce@unionchurch.com

Made in the USA
Middletown, DE
23 December 2022